Easy Sheet Music For Alto Saxophone With Alto Saxophone & Piano Duets Book 1

Michael Shaw

Copyright © 2015 Michael Shaw. All rights reserved. Including the right to reproduce this book or portions thereof, in any form. No part of this text may be reproduced in any form without the express written permission of the author.

Music Arrangements. All music arrangements in this book by **Michael Shaw**
Copyright © 2015

ISBN: 1517025338
ISBN-13: 978-1517025335

www.mikesmusicroom.co.uk

Contents

Introduction	
Merrily We Roll Along: Alto Saxophone	1
Merrily We Roll Along: Alto Saxophone & Piano	2
Lightly Row: Alto Saxophone	4
Lightly Row: Alto Saxophone & Piano	5
Lullabye: Alto Saxophone	7
Lullabye: Alto Saxophone & Piano	8
Barcarolle: Alto Saxophone	10
Barcarolle: Alto Saxophone & Piano	11
Amazing Grace: Alto Saxophone	14
Amazing Grace: Alto Saxophone & Piano	15
The New World Symphony: Alto Saxophone	17
The New World Symphony: Alto Saxophone & Piano	18
Beautiful Dreamer: Alto Saxophone	20
Beautiful Dreamer: Alto Saxophone & Piano	21
Michael Row The Boat Ashore: Alto Saxophone	23
Michael Row The Boat Ashore: Alto Saxophone & Piano	24
When The Saints Go Marching In: Alto Saxophone	26
When The Saints Go Marching In: Alto Saxophone & Piano	27
The Entertainer: Alto Saxophone	30
The Entertainer: Alto Saxophone & Piano	31
About The Author	34

Introduction

The sheet music in this book has been arranged for Alto Saxophone. There are two versions of every piece in this book. The first version is an Alto Saxophone only arrangement, the second version is a Saxophone and piano accompaniment arrangement. Both versions are for beginners and easy to play. The piano parts in this book can be played on a piano, keyboard or organ.

As well as playing duets with piano in this book you can also play together in a duet or ensemble with other instruments with an easy sheet music book for that instrument. All arrangements are the same and keys are adjusted for B flat, E flat, F and C instruments so everything sounds correct. Piano parts for all instrument books are in the same key.

To get a book for your instrument choose from the *Easy Sheet Music Book 1 with Piano Duets* series. Instruments in this series include, Clarinet, Trumpet, Alto Saxophone, Tenor Saxophone, Flute, French Horn and Trombone.

Author Page US
amazon.com/Michael-Shaw/e/B00FNVFJGQ/

Author Page UK
amazon.co.uk/Michael-Shaw/e/B00FNVFJGQ/

Merrily We Roll Along
Alto Sax

Traditional

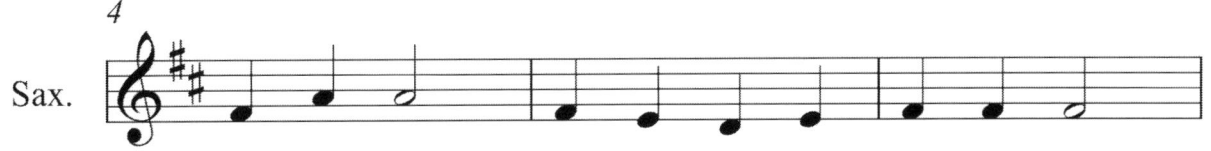

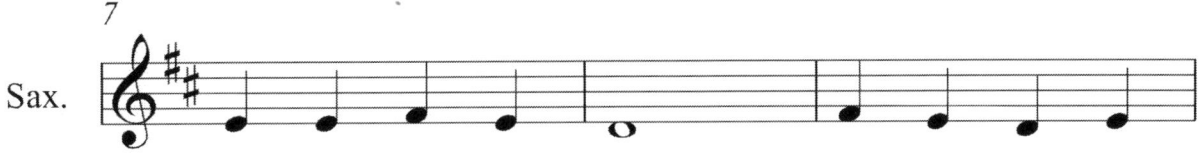

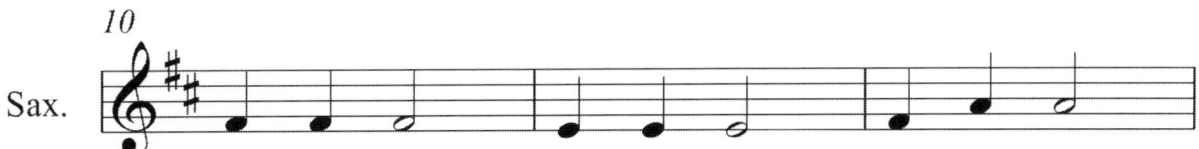

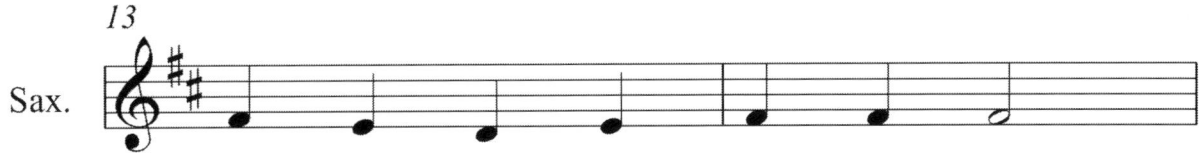

Merrily We Roll Along

Alto Sax & Piano

Traditional

Lightly Row
Alto Sax
Traditional

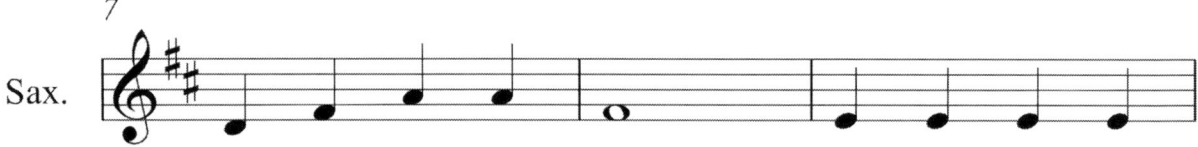

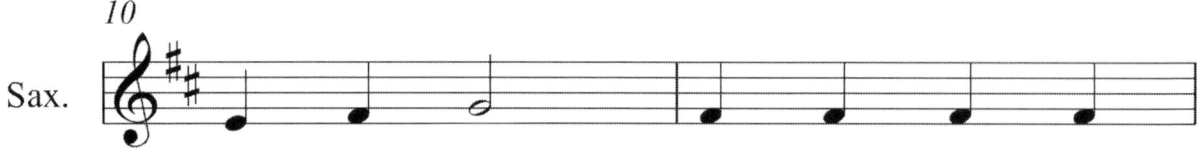

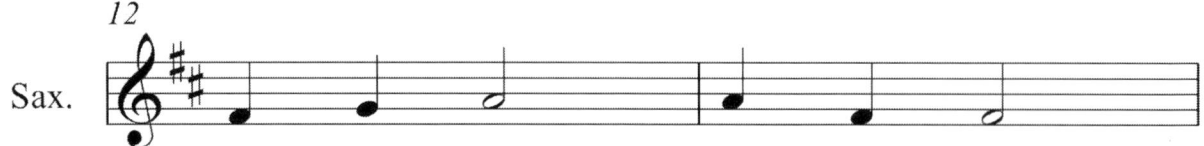

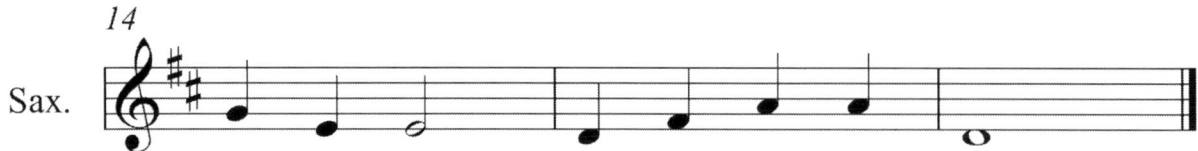

Lightly Row
Alto Sax & Piano

Traditional

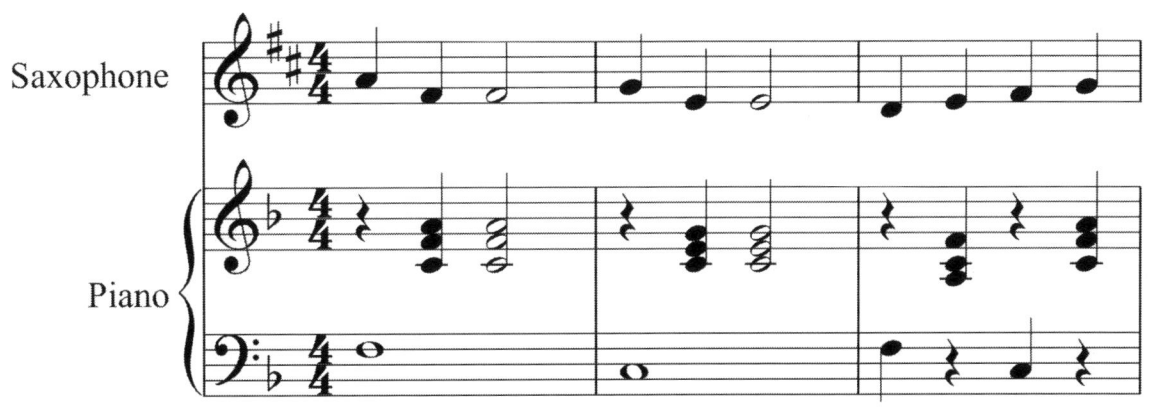

Lullabye
Alto Sax
Brahms

Lullabye

Alto Sax & Piano

Brahms

Barcarolle
Alto Sax

Jacques Offenbach

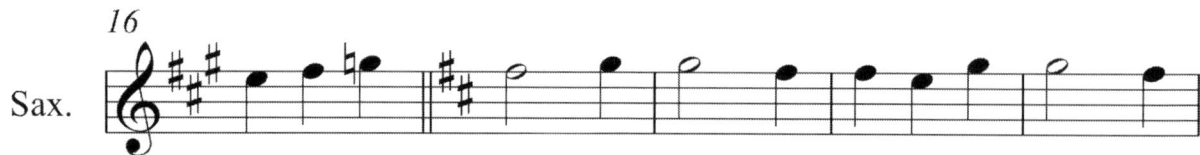
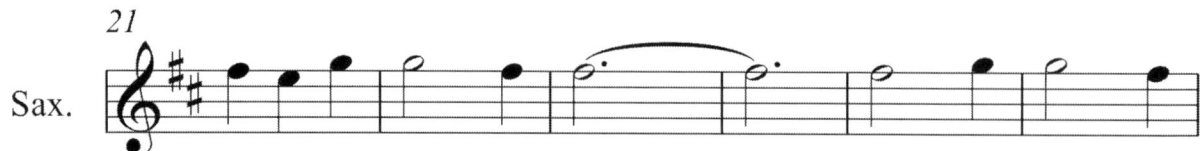

Barcarolle
Alto Sax & Piano

Jacques Offenbach

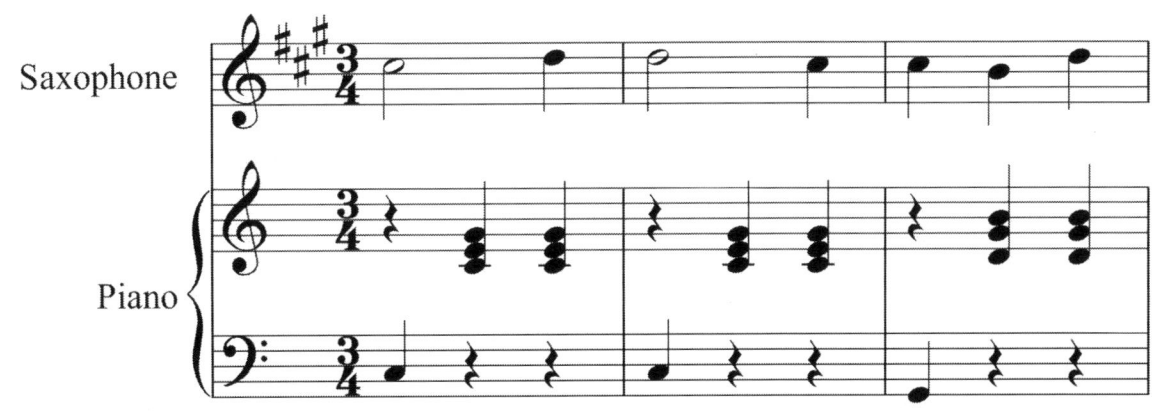

Amazing Grace
Alto Sax

John Newton

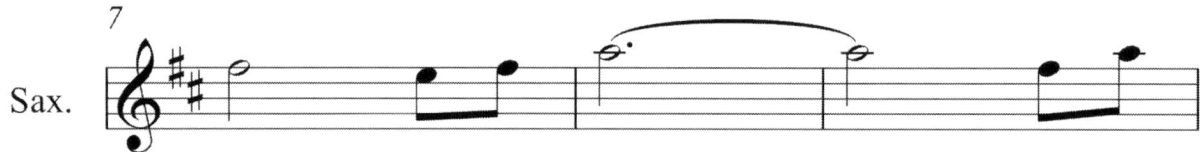

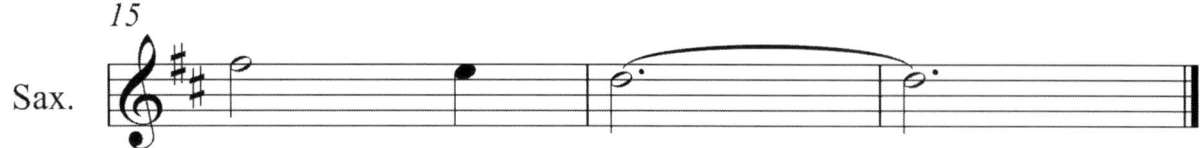

Amazing Grace
Alto Sax & Piano

John Newton

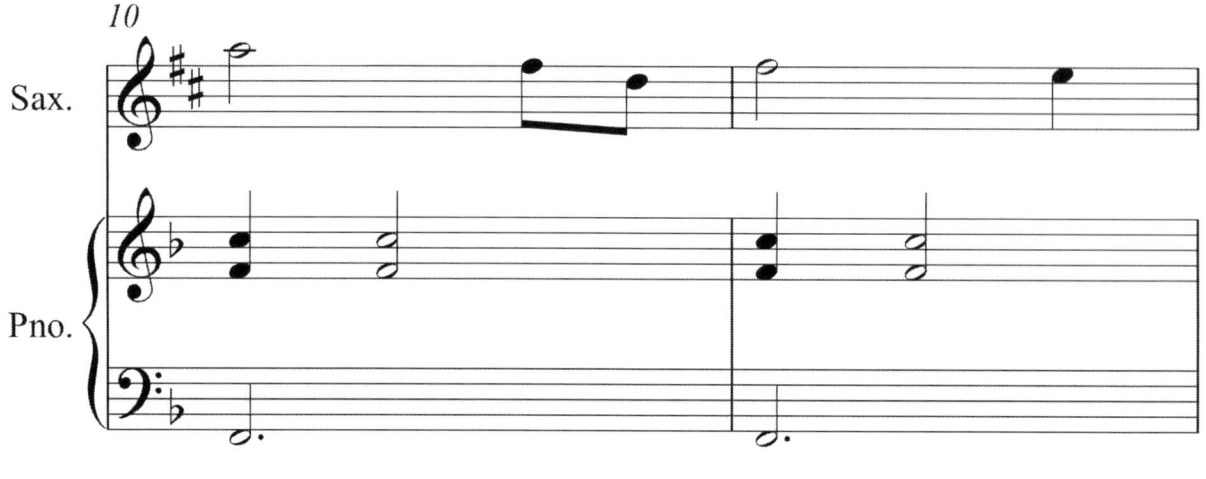

The New World Symphony

Largo

Alto Sax

Antonin Dvorak

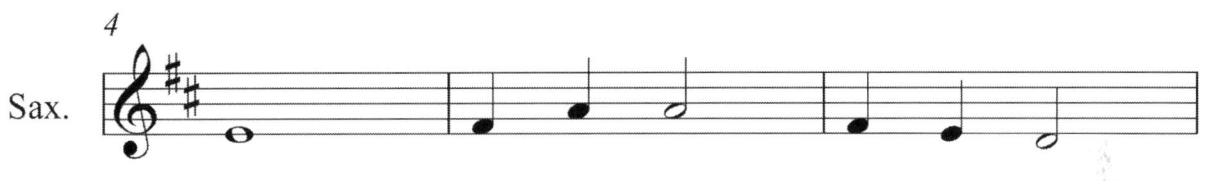
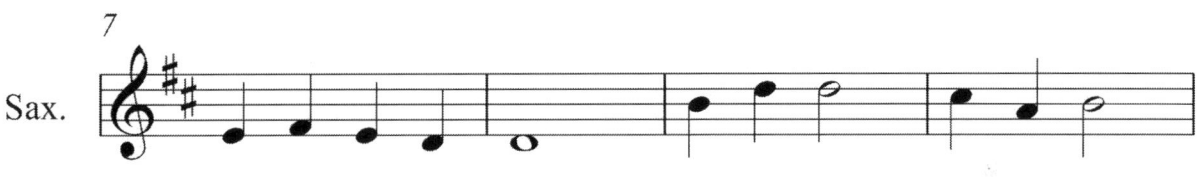

The New World Symphony

Largo

Antonin Dvorak

Alto Sax & Piano

Beautiful Dreamer

Alto Sax

Stephen Collins Foster

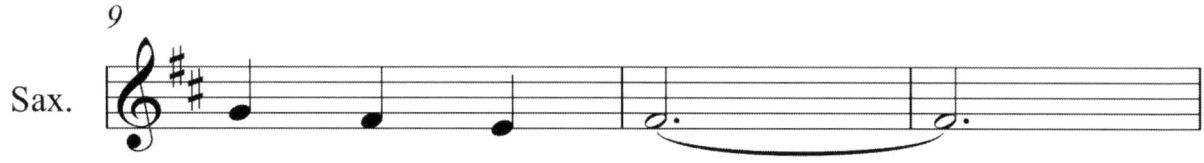

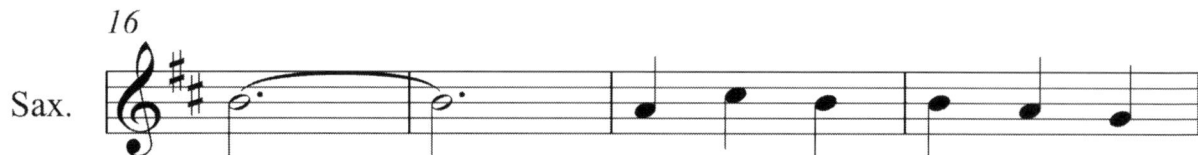

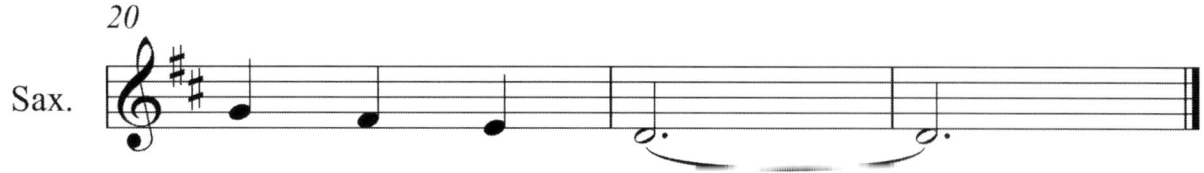

Beautiful Dreamer
Alto Sax & Piano
Stephen Collins Foster

Michael Row The Boat Ashore

Alto Sax

Traditional

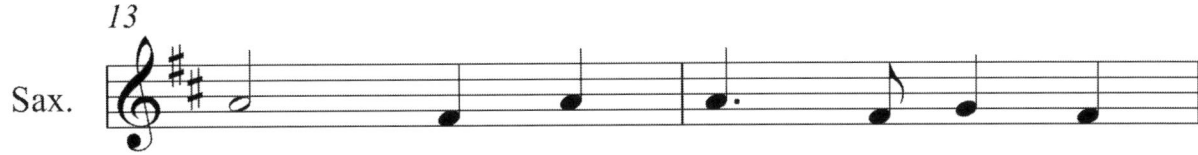

Michael Row The Boat Ashore
Alto Sax & Piano

Traditional

25

When The Saints Go Marching In

Alto Sax
Traditional

When The Saints Go Marching In
Alto Sax & Piano
Traditional

27

The Entertainer
Alto Sax

1902 - Scott Joplin

The Entertainer
Alto Sax & Piano

1902 - Scott Joplin

About the Author

Mike works as a professional musician and keyboard music teacher. Mike has been teaching piano, electronic keyboard and electric organ for over thirty years and as a keyboard player worked in many night clubs and entertainment venues.

Mike has also branched out in to composing music and has written and recorded many new royalty free tracks which are used worldwide in TV, film and internet media applications. Mike is also proud of the fact that many of his students have gone on to be musicians, composers and teachers in their own right.

You can connect with Mike at:

Facebook
facebook.com/keyboardsheetmusic

Soundcloud
soundcloud.com/audiomichaeld

YouTube
youtube.com/user/pianolessonsguru

I hope this book has helped you with your music, if you have received value from it in any way, then I'd like to ask you for a favour: would you be kind enough to leave a review for this book on Amazon? It'd be greatly appreciated!

Thank You
Michael Shaw

Made in the USA
Monee, IL
12 May 2021